Corel WordPerfect Keyboard Shortcuts

By

U. C-Abel Books.

Published by U. C-Abel Books

All Rights Reserved

First Edition: 2017

ISBN-13: 978-1544038711
ISBN-10: 1544038712

Published by U. C-Abel Books.

Table of Contents

Acknowledgement.

We return all glory to God Almighty for enabling us to bring this work to this point.

We sincerely appreciate the great company called Corel Corporation for their hard work and way of reasoning in terms of providing their customers with helpful programs and resources, and for helping us with some of the tips and keyboard shortcuts included in this book. We also remember our lovely readers who are never tired of reading our publications.

We really wish you well.

Dedication

We pleasurably dedicate this title to every Corel WordPerfect user all over the world.

Introduction

After thinking of how to help computer users become more productive in their operation of computers and various fields, it came to our knowledge that there is a smart option many computer users ignore easily and that part has a high yielding capacity that is known to just few people.

We went into a deep research to broaden our knowledge of key combination and found it very helpful, then we started this series "Shortcut Matters" including tips, techniques, keyboard shortcuts, and packaging the title in a way it will attract readers and get a high rating class.

As people who love keyboard shortcuts we treat each topic plainly in an easy-to-read way even to the understanding of a lay man.

Relax and make your mind ready for learning as we go.

What to Know Before You Begin.

General Notes.

1. Most of the keyboard shortcuts you will see in this book refer to the U.S. keyboard layout. Keys for other layouts might not correspond exactly to the keys on a U.S. keyboard. Keyboard shortcuts for laptop computers might also differ.

2. It is important to note that when using shortcuts to perform any command, you should make sure the target area is active, if not, you may get a wrong result. Example, if you want to highlight all texts you must make sure the text field is active and if an object, make sure the object area is active. The active area is always known by the location where the cursor of your computer blinks.

3. On a Mac keyboard, the Command key is denoted with the ⌘symbol.

4. If a function key doesn't work on your Mac as you expect it to, press the Fn key in addition to the function key. If you don't want to press the Fn key every time, you can change your Apple system preferences.

5. The plus (+) sign that comes in the middle of keyboard shortcuts simply means the keys are meant to be combined or held down together not to

be added as one of the shortcut keys. In a case where plus sign is needed; it will be duplicated (++).

6. Many keyboards assign special functions to function keys, by default. To use the function key for other purposes, you have to press Fn+the function key.

7. For keyboard shortcuts in which you press one key immediately followed by another key, the keys are separated by a comma (,).

8. For chapters that have more than one topic, search for "A fresh topic" to see the beginning of a topic, and "End of Topic" to see the end of a topic.

9. It is also important to note that the keyboard shortcuts listed in this book are to be used in Corel WordPerfect.

10. To get more information on this title visit ucabelbooks.wordpress.com and search the site using keywords related to it.

11. Our chief website is under construction.

Some Short Forms You Will Find in This Book and Their Full Meaning.

Here are short forms used in this Corel Word Perfect Keyboard Shortcuts book and their full meaning.

1. Win - Windows logo key
2. Tab - Tabulate Key
3. Shft - Shift Key
4. Prt sc - Print Screen
5. Num Lock - Number Lock Key
6. F - Function Key
7. Esc - Escape Key
8. Ctrl - Control Key
9. Caps Lock - Caps Lock Key
10. Alt - Alternate Key

CHAPTER 1.

Fundamental Knowledge of Keyboard Shortcuts.

Without the existence of the keyboard, there wouldn't have been anything like keyboard shortcuts so in this chapter we will learn a little about the computer keyboard before moving to keyboard shortcuts.

1. Definition of Computer Keyboard.

This is an input device that is used to send data to computer memory.

Sketch of a Keyboard

1.1 Types of Keyboard.

i. Standard (Basic) Keyboard.

ii. Enhanced (Extended) Keyboard.

i. **Standard Keyboard:** This is a keyboard designed during the 1800s for mechanical typewriters with just 10 function keys (F keys) placed at the left side of it.

ii. **Enhanced Keyboard:** This is the current 101 to 102-key keyboard that is included in almost all the personal computers (PCs) of nowadays, which has 12 function keys, usually at the top side of it.

Function Keys

Numeric Keys

Alphabetic keys

1.2 Segments of the keyboard

- Numeric keys.
- Alphabetic keys.
- Punctuation keys.
- Windows Logo key.
- Function keys.
- Special keys.

Numeric Keys: Numeric keys are keys with numbers from **0 - 9**.

Alphabetic Keys: These are keys that have alphabets on them, ranging from **A** to **Z**.

Punctuation Keys: These are keys of the keyboard used for punctuation, examples include comma, full stop, colon, question marks, hyphen, etc.

Windows Logo Key: A key on Microsoft Computer keyboard with its logo displayed on it. Search for this on your keyboard.

Apple Key: This also known as Command key is a modifier key that you can find on an Apple keyboard. It usually has the image of an apple or command logo on it. Search for this on your Apple keyboard

Function Keys: These are keys that have **F** on them which are usually combined with other keys. They are F1 - F12, and are also in the class called *Special Keys*.

Special Keys: These are keys that perform special functions. They include: Tab, Ctrl, Caps lock, Insert, Prt sc, alt gr, Shift, Home, Num lock, Esc, and many others. Special keys differ according to the type of computer involved. In some keyboard layout, especially laptops, the keys that turn the speaker on/off, the one that increases/decreases volume, the key that turns the computer Wifi on/off are also special keys.

Other Special Keys Worthy of Note.

Enter Key: This is located at the right-hand corner of most keyboards. It is used to send messages to the computer to execute commands, in most cases it is used to mean "Ok" or "Go".

Escape Key (ESC): This is the first key on the upper left of most keyboards. It is used to cancel routines, close menus and select options such as **Save** according to circumstances.

Control Key (CTRL): It is located on the bottom row of the left and right hand side of the keyboard. They also work with the function keys to execute commands using Keyboard shortcuts (key combinations).

Alternate Key (ALT): It is located on the bottom row also of some keyboard, very close to the CTRL key on both side of the keyboard. It enables many editing functions to be accomplished by using some keystroke combinations on the keyboard.

Shift Key: This adds to the roles of function keys. In addition, it enables the use of alternative function of a particular button (key), especially, those with more than one function on a key. E.g. use of capital letters, symbols, and numbers.

1.3. Selecting/Highlighting With Keyboard.

This is a highlighting method or style where data is selected using the computer keyboard instead of a computer mouse.

To do this:

- Move your cursor to the text or object you want to highlight, make sure that area is active,
- Hold down the shift key with one finger,
- Then use another finger to move the arrow key that points to the direction you want to highlight.

1.4 The Operating Modes Of The Keyboard.

Just like the computer mouse, keyboard has two operating modes. The two modes are Text Entering Mode and Command Mode.

a. **Text Entering Mode:** this mode gives the operator/user the opportunity to type text.
b. **Command Mode:** this is used to command the operating system/software/application to execute commands in certain ways.

2. Ways To Improve In Your Typing Skill.

1. Put Your Eyes Off The Keyboard.

This is the aspect of keyboard usage that many don't find funny because they always ask. "How can I put my eyes off the keyboard when I am running away from the occurrence of errors on my file?" My aim is to be fast, is this not going to slow me down?

Of course, there will be errors and at the same time your speed will slow down but the motive behind the introduction to this method is to make you faster than you are. Looking at your keyboard while you type can make you get a sore neck, it is better you learn to touch type because the more you type with your eyes fixed on the screen instead of the keyboard, the faster you become.

An alternative to keeping your eyes off your keyboard is to use the *"Das Keyboard Ultimate"*.

2. Errors Challenge You

It is better to fail than to not try at all. Not trying at all is an attribute of the weak and lazybones. When you make mistakes, try again because errors are opportunities for improvement.

3. Good Posture (Position Yourself Well).

Do not adopt an awkward position while typing. You should get everything on your desk organized or arranged before sitting to type. Your posture while typing contributes to your speed and productivity.

4. Practice

Here is the conclusion of everything said above. You have to practice your shortcuts constantly. The practice alone is a way of improvement. "Practice brings improvement". Practice always.

2.1 Software That Will Help You Improve Your Typing Skill.

There are several Software programs for typing that both kids and adults can use for their typing skill. Here is a list of software that can help you improve in your typing: Mavis Beacon, Typing Instructor, Mucky Typing Adventure, Rapid Tying Tutor, Letter Chase Tying Tutor, Alice Touch Typing Tutor and many more. Personally, I love Mavis Beacon.

To learn typing using MAVIS BEACON, install Mavis Beacon software to your computer, start with keyboard lesson, then move to games. Games like **Penguin Crossing, Creature Lab**, or **Space Junk** will help you become a professional in typing. Typing and keyboard shortcuts work hand-in-hand.

Sketch of a computer mouse

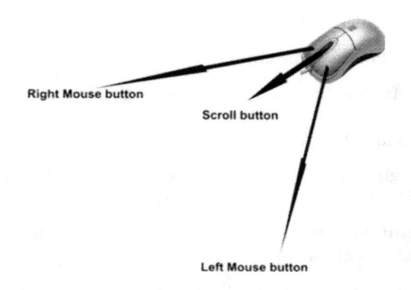

Right Mouse button

Scroll button

Left Mouse button

3. Mouse:

This is an oval-shaped portable input device with three buttons for scrolling, left clicking, and right clicking that enables work to be done effectively on a computer. The plural form of mouse is mice.

3.1 Types of Computer Mouse

- Mechanical Mouse.
- Optical Mechanical Mouse (Optomechanical).
- Laser Mouse.
- Optical Mouse.

- BlueTrack Mouse.

3.2 Forms of Clicking:

Left Clicking: This is the process of clicking the left side button of the mouse. It can also be called *clicking* without the addition of *left*.

Right Clicking: It is the process of clicking the right side button of a computer mouse.

Double Clicking: It is the process of clicking the left side button two times (twice) and immediately.

Triple Clicking: It is the process of clicking the left side button three times (thrice) and immediately.

Double clicking is used to select a word while triple clicking is used to select a sentence or paragraph.

Scroll Button: It is the little key attached to the mouse that looks like a tiny wheel. It takes you up and down a page when moved.

3.3 Mouse Pad: This is a small soft mat that is placed under the mouse to make it have a free movement.

3.4 Laptop Mouse Touchpad

This unlike the mouse we explained above is not external, rather it is inbuilt (comes with the laptop computer). With the presence of a laptop mouse touchpad, an external mouse is not needed to use a laptop, except in a case where it is malfunctioning or the operator prefers to use external one for some reasons.

The laptop mouse touchpad is usually positioned at the end of the keyboard section of a laptop computer. It is rectangular in shape with two buttons positioned below it. The two buttons/keys are used for left and right clicking just like the external mouse. Some laptops come with four mouse keys. Two placed above the mouse for left and right clicking and two other keys placed below it for the same function.

4. Definition Of Keyboard Shortcuts.

Keyboard shortcuts are defined as a series of keys, most times with combination that execute tasks which typically involve the use of mouse or other input devices.

5. Why You Should Use Shortcuts.

1. One may not be able to use a computer mouse easily because of disability or pain.

2. One may not be able to see the mouse pointer as a result of vision impairment, in such case what will the person do? The answer is SHORTCUT.

3. Research has made it known that Extensive mouse usage is related to Repetitive Syndrome Injury (RSI) greatly than the use of keyboard.

4. Keyboard shortcuts speed up computer users, making learning them a worthwhile effort.

5. When performing a job that requires precision, it is wise that you use the keyboard instead of mouse, for instance, if you are dealing with Text Editing, it is better you handle it using keyboard shortcuts than spending more time doing it with your computer mouse alone.

6. Studies calculate that using keyboard shortcuts allows working 10 times faster than working with the mouse. The time you spend looking for the mouse and then getting the cursor to the position you want is lost! Reducing your work duration by 10 times gives you greater results.

5.1 Ways To Become A Lover Of Shortcuts.

1. Always have the urge to learn new shortcut keys associated with the programs you use.
2. Be happy whenever you learn a new shortcut.
3. Try as much as you can to apply the new shortcuts you learnt.

4. Always bear it in mind that learning new shortcuts is worth it.

5. Always remember that the use of keyboard shortcuts keeps people healthy while performing computer activities.

5.2 How To Learn New Shortcut Keys

1. Do a research on them: quick references (a cheat sheet comprehensively compiled like ours) can go a long way to help you improve.

2. Buy applications that show you keyboard shortcuts every time you execute an action with mouse.

3. Disconnect your mouse if you must learn this fast.

4. Read user manuals and help topics (Whether offline or online).

5.3 Your Reward For Knowing Shortcut Keys.

1. You will get faster unimaginably.

2. Your level of efficiency will increase.

3. You will find it easy to use.

4. Opportunities are high that you will become an expert in what you do.

5. You won't have to go for **Office button**, click **New,** click **Blank and Recent**, and click **Create** just to insert a fresh/blank page. **Ctrl +N** takes care of that in a second.

A Funny Note: Keyboarding and Mousing are in a marital union with Keyboarding being the head, so it will be unfair for anybody to put asunder between them.

5.4 Why We Emphasize On The Use of Shortcuts.

You may never leave your mouse completely unless you are ready to make your brain a box of keyboard shortcuts which will really be frustrating, just imagine yourself learning all shortcuts that go with the programs you use and their various versions. You shouldn't learn keyboard shortcuts that way.

Why we are emphasizing on the use of shortcuts is because mouse usage is becoming unusually common and unhealthy, too. So we just want to make sure both are combined so you can get fast, productive and healthy in your computer activities. All you need to know is just the most important ones associated with the programs you use.

CHAPTER 2.

15 (Fifteen) Special Keyboard Shortcuts.

The fifteen special keyboard shortcuts are fifteen (15) shortcuts every computer user should know.

The following is a list of keyboard shortcuts every computer user should know:

1. **Ctrl + A:** Control A, highlights or selects everything you have in the environment where you are working.

   *If you are like **"Wow, the content of this document is large and there is no time to select all of it, besides, it's going to mount pressure on my computer?"** Using the mouse for this is an outdated method of handling a task like selecting all, Ctrl+A will take care of that in a second.*

2. **Ctrl + C:** Control C copies any highlighted or selected element within the work environment.

   Saves the time and stress which would have been used to right click and click again just to copy. Use ctrl+c.

3. **Ctrl + N:** Control N opens a new window or file.

   Instead of clicking **File**, **New**, **blank/ template** *and another* **click**, *just press* ***Ctrl + N*** *and a fresh page or window will appear instantly.*

4. **Ctrl + O:** Control O opens a new program.

   Use ctrl +O when you want to locate / open a file or program.

5. **Ctrl + P:** Control P prints the active document.

   Always use this to locate the printer dialog box, and thereafter print.

6. **Ctrl + S:** Control S saves a new document or file and changes made by the user.

   Please stop! Don't use the mouse. Just press Ctrl+S and everything will be saved.

7. **Ctrl +V:** Control V pastes copied elements into the active area of the program in use.

Using ctrl+V in a case like this Saves the time and stress of right clicking and clicking again just to paste.

8. **Ctrl + W:** Control W is used to close the page you are working on when you want to leave the work environment.

    "There is a way Debby does this without using the mouse. Oh my God, why didn't I learn it then?" Don't worry, I have the answer. Debby presses Ctrl+W to close active windows.

9. **Ctrl + X:** Control X cuts elements (making the elements to disappear from their original place). The difference between cutting and deleting elements is that in Cutting, what was cut doesn't get lost permanently but prepares itself so that it can be pasted on another location defined by the user.

    *Use ctrl+x when you think **"this shouldn't be here and I can't stand the stress of retyping or redesigning it on the rightful place it belongs"**.*

10. **Ctrl + Y:** Control Y undoes already done actions.

Ctrl+Z brought back what you didn't need? Press Ctrl+ Y to remove it again.

11. **Ctrl + Z:** Control Z redoes actions.
Can't find what you typed now or a picture you inserted, it suddenly disappeared or you mistakenly removed it? Press Ctrl+Z to bring it back.

12. **Alt + F4:** Alternative F4 closes active windows or items.

*You don't need to move the mouse in order to close an active window, just press **Alt + F4**. Also use it when you are done or you don't want somebody who is coming to see what you are doing.*

13. **Ctrl + F6:** Control F6 Navigates between open windows, making it possible for a user to see what is happening in windows that are active.
Are you working in Microsoft Word and want to find out if the other active window where your browser is loading a page is still progressing? Use Ctrl + F6.

14. **F1:** This displays the help window.

*Is your computer malfunctioning? Use **F1** to find help when you don't know what next to do.*

15. **F12:** This enables user to make changes to an already saved document.

    F12 is the shortcut to use when you want to change the format in which you saved your existing document, password it, change its name, change the file location or destination, or make other changes to it. It will save you time.

Note: The Control (Ctrl) key on Windows and Linux operating system is the same thing as Command (Cmmd) key on a Macintosh computer. So if you replace Control with Command key on a Mac computer for the special shortcuts listed above, you will get the same result.

CHAPTER 3.

Tips, Tricks, Techniques, and Keyboard Shortcuts for use in Corel Word Perfect.

About the program: This is a word processing application just like Microsoft Word, OpenOffice Writer, etc.

A fresh topic ⌐↳

Assigning the Signature Block Macro to a Keystroke.

It doesn't take long for the process of playing your favorite macros from the Play Macro dialog box to become tedious. That's when you start wishing there was a faster way to play a macro. There is a faster way – you can assign a macro to a keystroke, like Alt+K for example.

Click **Tools** > **Settings** > **Customize**. In the Customize settings dialog box, click the **Keyboards** tab. Click **Edit** to assign the macro to the current keyboard. In the **Choose a Shortcut Key** list, select a key in the list (i.e. Alt+K) to which you want to assign the signature block macro (see Figure 6). Click the **Macros** tab. Click **Assign Macro to Key**. In the Select macro dialog box, select the signature block macro. Click **Select** to assign the signature block macro to the keystroke. Click **OK** > **Close** > **Close.**

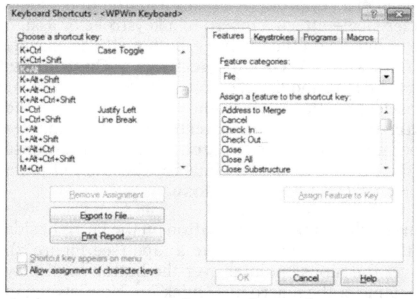

Assign your most frequently-used macros to a keystroke combination for quick access.

A fresh topic ⌐↳

Assigning the Signature Block Macro to a Toolbar Button.

You can also assign your macro to a toolbar button instead of a keystroke. It's really a matter of personal preference – attach a macro to a keystroke or assign it to a button on the toolbar – both methods provide fast access. Click **Tools > Settings > Customize**. Click **Edit** to modify the currently selected toolbar (or select another toolbar, then click Edit). Click the **Macros** tab. Click **Add Macro**. Select the signature block macro, then click **Select**. Click **No** in response to the prompt to save the macro with the full path, then click **OK > Close > Close**.

You should now see a new button on the far right side of the toolbar that looks like a tape (see Figure 7). Hover the mouse pointer over the button to display the name of the macro in a QuickTip. Now, switch to a blank document and try out the new toolbar button!

Macro buttos

Macro buttons are added to the far right side of a toolbar by default.

End of Topic.

A fresh topic

Macros Included with WordPerfect.

Macro	Description
checkbox.wcm	Inserts a check box in the document that you can click to add or remove a check mark.
closeall.wcm	Closes all open documents and prompts you to save the modified ones.
ctrlm.wcm	Activates the macro command browser.
cvtdocs.wcm	Lets you convert multiple documents from another document type to WordPerfect format.

dcconvert.wcm	Converts "whole word" drop caps to "number of characters" drop caps for conversion to Microsoft Word.
endfoot.wcm	Converts endnotes to footnotes in the document or selected text. To run this macro, your cursor must be outside of the footnote or endnote box (that is, your cursor must be in the main body of the page).
expndall.wcm	Expands all QuickWords in the document.
filestmp.wcm	Places the filename and path of the current document in a header or footer.
flipenv.wcm	Creates an envelope rotated 180 degrees (text is upside down). On printers with a large trailing margin, this lets you print the return address 0.25" from the edge.
footend.wcm	Converts footnotes to endnotes in the document or in selected text.
parabrk.wcm	Inserts symbols or small graphics as paragraph breaks. The graphics are centered on the blank line between paragraphs.
pleading.wcm	Creates lines and numbers for pleading documents.

prompts.wcm	Helps you create prompts for automated templates.
reverse.wcm	Creates white text on black background (or uses other color combinations) in selected text or table cells.
saveall.wcm	Prompts you to save open documents.
wp_org.wcm	Creates an organization chart in WordPerfect.
wp_pr.wcm	Sends a WordPerfect outline to Presentations.

End of Topic.

A fresh topic

Sharing Documents Between WordPerfect® Office and Microsoft® Office.

A question that WordPerfect® Office users often ask is, "Can I share my WordPerfect Office documents with Microsoft® Office users?" The answer, in brief, is, "Yes!" You can share your files with them and they can share their files with you.

For example, to share a WordPerfect® document with a Microsoft® Word user, you must save the WordPerfect document as a Microsoft Word file. The saving process automatically converts the document to the Microsoft Word format. The same process applies when saving Quattro Pro® files to Microsoft® Excel and Presentations™ files to Microsoft® PowerPoint®.

Save as type:	MS Word 2007-2016 (*.docx)
	MS Word 4.0 (*.doc)
	MS Word 5.0 (*.doc)
	MS Word 5.5 (*.doc)
	MS Word 6.0/7.0 for Windows (*.doc)
	MS Word 97/2000/2002/2003 (*.doc)
	MS Word for Windows 1.0 (*.doc)
	MS Word for Windows 1.1 (*.doc)
	MS Word for Windows 1.1a (*.doc)
	MS Word for Windows 1.2/1.2a (*.doc)
	MS Word for Windows 2.0 (*.doc)
	MS Word for Windows 2.0a (*.doc)
	MS Word for Windows 2.0b (*.doc)
	MS Word for Windows 2.0c (*.doc)
	MultiMate 3.3 (*.doc)

In WordPerfect, the File Type list box displays the Microsoft Word versions you can save to.

In addition, if you receive a file created in a Microsoft Office application, all you need to do is open it in the corresponding WordPerfect Office application. For example, if you are opening a Microsoft Excel file in Quattro Pro, the opening process automatically converts the file to the Quattro Pro format.

File type: 📊 Microsoft Excel (''*.xls'' ''*.xlsx'' ''*.xlsm'') ⌄

In Quattro Pro, you can open files created in most versions of Microsoft Excel.

If you modify the file and you want others to view the changes in Microsoft Excel, then you need to save the file as a Microsoft Excel file. If you don't specify the Microsoft Excel format when saving, the file is saved as a Quattro Pro file by default. Again, the same process applies when modifying Microsoft Excel files in Quattro Pro and Microsoft PowerPoint files in Presentations.

You can, however, specify that the default format when saving files is set to a Microsoft file format. For example, in WordPerfect, you can choose to automatically save files in the same file format in which the file was opened. In Quattro Pro, you can specify to automatically save all files to the Microsoft Excel file format.

To save a WordPerfect® Office file as a Microsoft® Office file

1. In WordPerfect, Quattro Pro, or Presentations, click File, Save as.
2. Choose the drive and folder where you want to save the file.
3. Type the filename in the Filename box.
4. Choose the appropriate Microsoft Office file format from the File type list box:
   •In WordPerfect, choose MS Word
   •In Quattro Pro, choose Microsoft Excel
   •In Presentations, choose MS PowerPoint
5. Click Save.

To open a file created in a Microsoft® Office application

1. In WordPerfect, Quattro Pro, or Presentations, click File, Open.
2. Choose the drive and folder where the Microsoft Office file is stored.
   If you can't see the file, choose All files from the File type box.
3. Click the Microsoft Office file.
4. Click Open.

To automatically save Microsoft® Word files opened in WordPerfect® to the Microsoft® Word format
1. Click Tools, Settings, Files.
2. On the Document page, enable the On save, keep the document's original file format check box.

To automatically save files opened in Quattro®
Pro® to the Microsoft® Excel format.
1. Click Tools, Settings.
2. In the list of categories, double-click
   Compatibility.
3. Choose XLS (or XLSX) from the Default file
   type list box.

End of Topic.

A fresh topic ⌐
     ⌐→

Using the Workspace Manager.

The Workspace Manager lets you simulate other
office productivity applications while using
WordPerfect® Office 12. For example, you can
simulate the Microsoft® Excel workspace while
using Quattro Pro® 12. A workspace is the user's
environment within an application. It encompasses
the document window and all visible components of
the application, such as menus, toolbars, and
buttons. It also includes the application's keyboard
shortcuts.

By letting you simulate an application that you may
be more familiar with, the Workspace Manager

reduces training costs and the time associated with learning a new application. For example, if you recently switched from Microsoft® Office, you may not be familiar with the keystrokes, menus, and toolbars of WordPerfect Office 12 applications.

While there are many similarities between the two suites, you may find it easier to simulate the Microsoft Office workspaces until you are more accustomed to working with WordPerfect Office 12. In an office environment, the Workspace Manager lets multiple users of the same computer easily switch back and forth between their preferred workspace.

The Workspace Manager positions WordPerfect Office 12 features, including toolbars and menu items, exactly where you would find the Microsoft Office equivalent. It also applies Microsoft Office keyboard shortcuts to WordPerfect Office 12 features — allowing you to quickly access the tools that you need.

WordPerfect Office 12 - Small Business Edition offers one-click access to the following workspaces:

Applicati on	WordPerfe ct® 12	Quatt ro Pro® 12	Presentatio ns™ 12

Availabl e workspa ces	WordPerfect Mode	Quattr o Pro Mode	Presentations Mode
	Microsoft Word Mode	Micros oft Excel Mode	Microsoft PowerPoint Mode
	WordPerfect Classic Mode (version 5.1)	Micros oft Excel Mode	
	Lotus 1-2-3 Mode		

If you're using a version other than WordPerfect Office 12 - Small Business Edition, your available workspace choices may differ.

When you first start a WordPerfect Office 12 application, the Workspace Manager displays by default. You can choose not to load the Workspace Manager at startup by disabling the Show at startup checkbox (see below). To access the Workspace Manager while using the applications, use the following instructions.

To simulate another word processing application in WordPerfect® 12

1. From the Tools menu, choose Workspace Manager.

2. In the Workspace Manager dialog box (see below), choose either of the following options:
   o WordPerfect Mode
   o Microsoft Word Mode/li>
   o WordPerfect Classic Mode (version 5.1)/li>
   o WordPerfect Legal Mode/li>
3. Click OK.

WordPerfect® 12

Choose the WordPerfect mode that you want to work in

- ⦿ WordPerfect Mode
- ○ Microsoft Word Mode
- ○ WordPerfect Classic Mode (version 5.1)
- ○ WordPerfect Legal Mode

The mode you choose changes the look of, and options found in, the WordPerfect workspace. To change the workspace mode during a WordPerfect session, click Tools > Workspace Manager.

☐ Show at startup

[OK] [Cancel] [Help]

To simulate another spreadsheet application in Quattro Pro® 12

1. From the Tools menu, choose Workspace Manager.

2. In the Options dialog box (see below), choose either of the following options:
   - Quattro Pro 12
   - Lotus 1-2-3
   - Microsoft Excel
3. Click OK.

To simulate the Microsoft® PowerPoint® workspace in Presentations™ 12

1. From the Tools menu, choose Workspace Manager.

2. In the Workspace Manager dialog box (see below), enable the Microsoft PowerPoint option.

3. Click OK.

Presentations 12

Choose the Presentations mode that you want to work in...

○ Presentations Mode
◉ Microsoft PowerPoint Mode

The mode you choose changes the look of, and options found in, the Presentations workspace. To change the workspace mode during a Presentations session, click Tools > Workspace Manager

☑ Show at startup   OK   Cancel   Help

End of Topic.

A fresh topic ⌐↳

WordPerfect Shortens the Road to File Conversion.

Suppose you need to convert a batch of Microsoft® Word files to WordPerfect®. How do you go about doing it? Do you open the files in WordPerfect one at a time? Opening files individually works fine if you are converting only one or two files. It's very time consuming, however, if you need to convert multiple files. Do you create a macro? You could, but, again, you probably have better things to do.

The options listed above describe the long road to file conversion, but you will be happy to know that there is a shortcut.

WordPerfect has another option for converting multiple files simultaneously: the WordPerfect® Office Conversion Utility. It can convert various types of files, such as Microsoft® Word files, to one of five WordPerfect file formats.

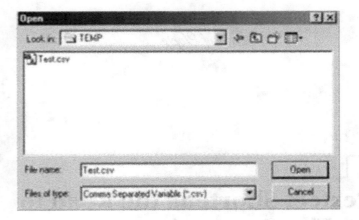

You can also open multiple files using a Comma-separated values (csv) file. The csv file needs to contain a list of the files, including their directory structure. This allows you to organize the files before converting them. For example, the csv option is useful if you need to convert some, but not all files, or if you want to select some but not all subfolders. Without using a csv file, you would have to manually add the files found in the different folders.

If you chose the standard installation of WordPerfect Office, the WordPerfect Office Conversion Utility should be available by default. If it's not available, you can add it by modifying the installation. Remember the WordPerfect® Office Conversion Utility the next time you need to convert a batch of files. Why take the long road when there is a shortcut.

To Install the WordPerfect® Office Conversion Utility.

1. Close any open applications.
2. On the Windows taskbar, click Start } Settings } Control panel.
3. Double-click the Add/Remove programs icon.
4. Choose WordPerfect Office 11 from the Currently installed programs list.
5. Click Change.
6. In the InstallShield wizard, enable the Modify option, and click Next.
7. In the list of features, open the WordPerfect Office 11 } Utilities category.

8. Click the icon next to the WordPerfect Conversion Utility item, and click This feature will be installed on local hard drive.
9. Click Next.
10. Click Install.

To Start the Conversion Utility.

- On the Windows taskbar, click Start} Programs } WordPerfect Office 11 } Utilities } Conversion utility.

To convert a multiple files to the WordPerfect® format

1. Click Add.
2. Choose the drive and folder where the files you want to convert are stored.
3. Click Add all.
   If you want to convert the files in the folders within the folder, enable the Include subfolders check box.
4. From the Convert to list box, choose a version of WordPerfect.

To convert an imported comma separated value (CSV) file into WordPerfect®

1. Click Import.
2. Click Add.

3. Choose the drive and folder where the CSV file is stored.
4. Click a file.
5. Click Open.
6. Click OK.

7. From the Convert to list box, choose a version of WordPerfect.

End of Topic.

A fresh topic ⌐

Publishing WordPerfect® Documents to PDF.

Do you need to share your WordPerfect® documents with people who don't have WordPerfect? If you do, you have the option of publishing documents to Portable Document Format (PDF). PDF format is useful when you want to distribute documents that are meant only for viewing and printing.

When publishing to PDF, you can choose one of three preset styles. The style settings are designed to optimize the PDF document for a specific method of distribution. The style you choose should correspond with how you plan to distribute the file.

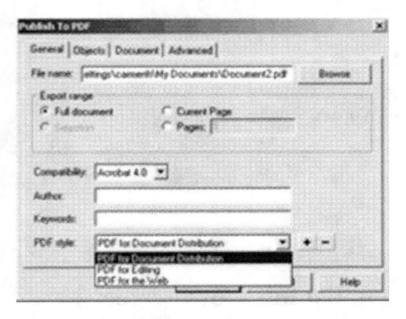

You can choose from three PDF styles.

For example, for most documents, you can choose the document distribution style because the settings are suitable for the average document. You can specify the Web style if you plan to post the file on a Web page; this optimizes the PDF file for viewing on the Web and it also reduces the file size. The editing style publishes the PDF file with all fonts and images at full resolution; this can be useful if you plan to edit the file using Adobe® Acrobat®.

The person receiving the PDF file can view or print it if they have Adobe® Reader® installed on their computer. If you want to view the PDF files you create before sending them to others, you also need to have Adobe Reader installed on your computer. If you don't have it, you can install it from WordPerfect Office 11 CD 2.

To publish the active document to PDF

1. Click File, Publish to PDF.

2. Click the General tab.

3. In the Export range area, enable one of the following options:

41

- Full document — publishes the entire file
- Current page — publishes the active page only
- Pages — publishes a portion of the file
- Selection — publishes selected text

4. From the PDF style list box, choose one of the following options:

- PDF for document distribution
- PDF for the Web
- PDF for editing

5. In the Filename list box, click Browse.

6. Choose the drive and folder where you want to save the file.

7. Type the filename in the Filename box.

8. Click Save.

To install Adobe® Reader®

1. Insert WordPerfect Office 11 CD 2 into the CD drive. If the Setup wizard does not start automatically, proceed to step 2; otherwise, proceed to step 6.

2. Click Start on the Windows® taskbar, and click

Run.

3. Type D:SETUP, where D is the letter that corresponds to the CD drive.

4. Double-click ExploreCD.exe.

5. Double-click intro.exe.

6. In the WordPerfect Office 11 CD 2 dialog box, click Adobe Acrobat Reader.

7. Follow the instructions in the Adobe Reader setup program.

End of Topic.

A fresh topic

Using the Conversion Utility.

The process of converting documents from other file formats has improved with each new release of WordPerfect. In version 11, there is a brand new conversion utility that will batch convert documents in other formats, so you don't have to do them one at a time. The list of formats is too long to include here, but suffice it to say that every known version of Microsoft Word is there as well as RTF, HTML, DIF, StarOffice, ANSI/ASCII, and WP for Mac. You can even convert CSV (comma separated value) files.

To start the conversion utility, click Start, (All) Programs, WordPerfect Office 11, Utilities, Conversion Utility. The first step is to select the files that you want to convert, so click the Add button. Choose the drive and folder where the files are stored. Select the file, then click Add, or, if you want to convert all of the files in this folder, click Add all.

Once you've built the list, select the version of WordPerfect that you want to convert the files to in the Convert to drop-down list. Notice that you can convert to DOS and Macintosh file formats. There are some options that you can set with regards to duplicate file names. Otherwise, choose OK to start the conversion.

If you wish to view and change the file name

options, click the Options button. In the Conversion Options dialog box, you can opt to create a log file of the conversion process. I find this extremely helpful when I'm converting a large number of files and I want to verify that the process went smoothly.

By default, the utility will save the converted files to the same folder. If you prefer, you can have the files saved in a different folder. You can also save a copy of the converted file as a CSV file, which could be used as an alternate if the conversion process doesn't go as well as you had hoped. Enable the Create a conversion file option, specify a drive and folder where you want to save the CSV file, then choose Save.

If you want more information on any of the conversion options, or if you want to view a complete list of file formats that can be converted with the utility, click the Help button to access the help topics.

End of Topic.

A fresh topic →

Using WordPerfect® Classic Mode.

WordPerfect® Classic mode lets you work in the familiar visual environment of Corel® WordPerfect® 5.1 and use its keystrokes.

The WordPerfect Classic mode environment emulates that of Corel WordPerfect 5.1 by modifying the WordPerfect environment. For example, in WordPerfect Classic mode some elements, such as the toolbars, property bar, horizontal scrollbar, and ruler, are not displayed by default; the page display shows document text in a window with minimal white space in the margins; the document color is blue; and the displayed text is gray, although it still prints black-on-white unless otherwise specified.

Before you can start working in the WordPerfect Classic mode environment, you must install it and enable it. If you want to perform functions using keystrokes that are based on Corel WordPerfect 5.1, you need to enable the Classic mode keyboard.

To install WordPerfect® Classic mode

1. Close any open applications.
2. On the Windows® taskbar, click Start, Settings, Control panel.
3. Double-click the Add/Remove programs icon.
4. Choose WordPerfect Office 11 from the Currently installed programs list.
5. Click Change.
6. In the InstallShield® wizard, enable the Modify option, and click Next.
7. In the list of features, open the WordPerfect Office 11, WordPerfect category.
8. Click the icon next to the WordPerfect Classic mode item, and click This feature will be installed on local hard drive.
9. Click Next.
10. Click Install.

To enable the Classic mode environment

1. In WordPerfect, click Tools, Settings, Display.
2. Click the Document tab.
3. Enable the Classic mode (WP 5.1) check box.

To enable the Classic mode keyboard

1. In WordPerfect, click Tools, Settings, Customize.
2. Click the Keyboards tab.
3. Choose from the Available keyboards list.

4. Click Select.

Installing Additional Templates

Templates are great timesavers. Imagine a collection of professionally designed documents– ready to use–all you have to do is fill in the blanks. That's what a template is. You can save hours of formatting if you take advantage of WordPerfect's templates.

A small collection of templates is installed when you install WordPerfect. You can see the list by choosing File, New From Project. Make sure WordPerfect appears in the drop-down list. Additional templates are available in a free download. Although the templates were written for WordPerfect 10, they will work just fine in WordPerfect 11.

The templates can be downloaded from OfficeCommunity.com in the Download Gallery section. To download a template or project zip file from OfficeCommunity.com, click the [download] link. When you are prompted, save the file to the \wordperfect office 11 emplate folder under the \program files tree.

You can also download them from Corel's FTP site at ftp://ftp.corel.com/pub/WordPerfect/wpwin/10/english/templates. To download a template, click the name of the template you are interested in. This opens that template's folder on the FTP server. Within each template's folder is a file named Template and Project - Read Me.htm. This file contains detailed information about installing the templates in WordPerfect.

There are some other extras on the ftp site. First, there is a Zip file called WP 10 Temp that contains all the template files so that you can download the whole collection at one time. Second, within each template category folder is a README file with instructions for installing. Third, there is a thumbnail folder in each category, containing a GIF file that shows you what each created project form might look like.

If you download a Zip file, extract the template files (.wpt and .ast) to the \wordperfect office 11 emplate folder under the \program files tree. Now, you're ready to add them into WordPerfect.

To install downloaded templates:

1. Choose File, New from Project to open the PerfectExpert dialog box.
2. Click the Options button, and then select Refresh Projects from the list. Click Yes to confirm.

On my system, the downloaded templates were stored in a WordPerfect 10 category, so if you don't see the new templates in the list, open the drop-down list of categories and select WordPerfect 10.

When you open one of the WordPerfect 10 templates, you may see a message stating that the PerfectExpert resource file couldn't be found. It's only a warning and you can ignore it.

Creating a Sheet of Identical Labels

You may already know how to use the Merge feature to create labels for a mass mailing, but did you know you can create a sheet of identical labels as well? You can print your own return address labels, business cards, or any other kind of label that you use often, with this method.

To create a sheet of identical labels:

1. Choose Format, Labels and select the label form. Create the first label.
2. Choose Tools, Merge.
3. Choose Form Document, Create Form Document, Use File in Active Window.
4. If the Associate Form and Data dialog box appears, choose No Association. Otherwise, choose Data Source, None in the Merge dialog box.
5. Choose Options, then type the number of labels on the page in the Number of Copies for Each Record text box.
6. Choose Merge.

The resulting document will contain a number of identical labels. If you flubbed the number of labels, don't worry. Just close this document, without saving, and try the merge again. When you are finished, save the label form for the next time you want to print these labels.

Protecting a File from Accidental Modification.

Most of us have "form" documents that we open and use to create a new document. Businesses usually have a collection of form letters so the correspondence leaving the company has a consistent appearance and tone. The trick is to remember to immediately save the new document under a new name, so the changes aren't accidentally saved to the "form" document. If you forget, you can easily save your changes, and alter the original.

There is a better way. You can designate a file to be "read-only". When you open a read-only file, you won't be allowed to save your changes to the original, so you have to save your changes to a new file. It is impossible to accidentally modify a file that has been set to read-only.

To designate a file as read-only, you must have saved the file to disk. You cannot have a copy of the file open in a WordPerfect window.

1. Choose File, Open.
2. Navigate to the file that you want to designate as read-only.
3. Right-click the file and choose Properties.
4. Place a check mark in the Read-only check box in the Attributes section.
5. Choose OK.

Note: To make changes to this original file, you'll have to reverse the process and remove the Read-only attribute. Be sure you set it back after you've finalized the new form document.

End of Topic.

A fresh topic ⌐⌐⌐

Working with Microsoft Word Users.

WordPerfect® Office makes it easy to share documents with Microsoft® Office users. WordPerfect has compatibility features that let you open and edit Microsoft® Word files. You can then save the file in the native file format of Microsoft Word, allowing for the sharing of files across applications. WordPerfect also lets you save any document in the Microsoft Word file format.

When you finish a document, you can e-mail it directly from WordPerfect.

To open a Microsoft® Word Document.

1. Click File > Open.

2. Choose the drive and folder where the Microsoft Word file is stored.
Choose Microsoft Word from the File type box.

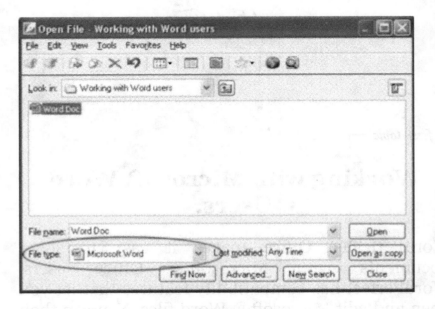

3. Click the Microsoft Word file.

4. Click Open.

To save a WordPerfect® Document as a Microsoft® Word Document.

1. Click File > Save as.

2. Choose the drive and folder where you want to save the file.

3. Type the filename in the File name box.

4. Choose an MS Word format from the File type list box.

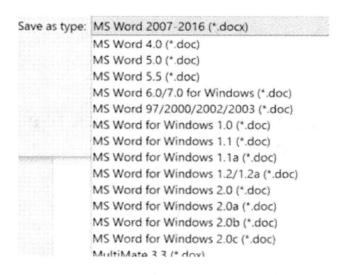

Save as type: MS Word 2007-2016 (*.docx)
MS Word 4.0 (*.doc)
MS Word 5.0 (*.doc)
MS Word 5.5 (*.doc)
MS Word 6.0/7.0 for Windows (*.doc)
MS Word 97/2000/2002/2003 (*.doc)
MS Word for Windows 1.0 (*.doc)
MS Word for Windows 1.1 (*.doc)
MS Word for Windows 1.1a (*.doc)
MS Word for Windows 1.2/1.2a (*.doc)
MS Word for Windows 2.0 (*.doc)
MS Word for Windows 2.0a (*.doc)
MS Word for Windows 2.0b (*.doc)
MS Word for Windows 2.0c (*.doc)
MultiMate 3.3 (* dox)

5. Click Save.

To e-mail a document from WordPerfect®

Click File > Send to > Mail recipient.

File Edit View Insert Format Table Tools Window Help
Send To   ▶   Mail Recipient

Your e-mail client opens, and a new mail message is created with the document as an attachment.

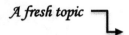

Common Keyboard Shortcuts for WordPerfect.

The following list is made up of keyboard shortcuts you can use to boost your productivity in Corel WordPerfect.

TASK	SHORTCUT
Bold	Ctrl-B
Copy	Ctrl-C
Center	Shift-F7
Cut	Ctrl-X
Close	Ctrl-F4
Dictionary	Alt-Ctrl-F1
Date	Ctrl-D
Document Map	Ctrl-Shift-M
Draft View	Ctrl-F5

Find & Replace	F2 or Ctrl-F
Find Next	Shift-F2
Find Previous	Alt-F2
Flush Right	Alt-F7
Font	F9
Generate	Ctrl-F9
Go To	Ctrl-G
Grammatik	Alt-Shift-F1
Graphic box edit	Shift-F11
Graphic, insert from File.	F11
Hard page	Ctrl-Shift-Enter
Help	F1
Hide Bars	Alt-Shift-F5
Horizontal Line	Ctrl-F11
Indent	F7
Indent, double	Ctrl-Shift-F7
Indent, hanging	Ctrl-F7
Justify, left	Ctrl-L
Justify, right.	Ctrl-R
Justify, center	Ctrl-E
Justify, full	Ctrl-J
Italics	Ctrl-I
Line, horizontal	Ctrl-F11
Line, vertical	Ctrl-Shift-F11
Macro Play	Alt-F10
Macro Record	Ctrl-F10
Margins	Ctrl-F8
Menu command	F10
Merge	Shift-F9

Customer's Page.

This page is for customers who enjoyed Corel WordPerfect Keyboard Shortcuts.

Dear beautiful customer, we will feel honoured to have you review this book if you enjoyed or found it useful. We also advise you to get the ebook copy of this book so as to access the numerous links in it. Thank you.

Download Our EBooks Today For Free.

In order to appreciate our customers, we have made some of our titles available at 0.00. They are totally free. Feel free to get a copy of the free titles.

Here are books we give to our customers free of charge:

(A) For Keyboard Shortcuts in Windows check:

Windows 7 Keyboard Shortcuts.

(B) For Keyboard Shortcuts in Office 2016 for Windows check:

Word 2016 Keyboard Shortcuts For Windows.

(C) For Keyboard Shortcuts in Office 2016 for Mac check:

OneNote 2016 Keyboard Shortcuts For Macintosh.

Follow this link to download any of the titles listed above for free.

Note: Feel free to download them from our website or your favorite bookstore today. Thank you.

Other Books By This Publisher.

<u>Note:</u> Titles for single programs under Shortcut Matters series are not part of this list.

S/N	Title	Series
Series A: Limits Breaking Quotes.		
1	<u>Discover Your Key Christian Quotes</u>	Limits Breaking Quotes
Series B: Shortcut Matters.		
1	<u>Windows 7 Shortcuts</u>	Shortcut Matters
2	<u>Windows 7 Shortcuts & Tips</u>	Shortcut Matters
3	<u>Windows 8.1 Shortcuts</u>	Shortcut Matters
4	<u>Windows 10 Shortcut Keys</u>	Shortcut Matters
5	<u>Microsoft Office 2007 Keyboard Shortcuts For Windows.</u>	Shortcut Matters
6	<u>Microsoft Office 2010 Shortcuts For Windows.</u>	Shortcut Matters
7	<u>Microsoft Office 2013 Shortcuts For Windows.</u>	Shortcut Matters
8	<u>Microsoft Office 2016 Shortcuts For Windows.</u>	Shortcut Matters
9	<u>Microsoft Office 2016 Keyboard Shortcuts For Macintosh.</u>	Shortcut Matters
10	<u>Top 11 Adobe Programs Keyboard Shortcuts</u>	Shortcut Matters
11	<u>Top 10 Email Service Providers Keyboard Shortcuts</u>	Shortcut Matters
12	<u>Hot Corel Programs Keyboard Shortcuts</u>	Shortcut Matters

13	Top 10 Browsers Keyboard Shortcuts	Shortcut Matters
14	Microsoft Browsers Keyboard Shortcuts.	Shortcut Matters
15	Popular Email Service Providers Keyboard Shortcuts	Shortcut Matters
16	Professional Video Editing with Keyboard Shortcuts.	Shortcut Matters
17	Popular Web Browsers Keyboard Shortcuts.	Shortcut Matters

Series C: Teach Yourself.

1	Teach Yourself Computer Fundamentals	Teach Yourself
2	Teach Yourself Computer Fundamentals Workbook	Teach Yourself

Series D: For Painless Publishing

1	Self-Publish it with CreateSpace.	For Painless Publishing
2	Where is my money? Now solved for Kindle and CreateSpace	For Painless Publishing
3	Describe it on Amazon	For Painless Publishing